COUNTRY BAKING

RECIPES

Delicious recipes for cakes, pies and tarts

With illustrations of country scenes by Terry Whitworth

SALMON

INDEX

Front Cover: Exmoor cottages at Selworthy, Somerset
Back Cover: Elmley Castle, Warwickshire
Title page: Cley Windmill, Norfolk

Printed and Published by Dorrigo, Manchester, England. © Copyright.

FLUFFY GINGER SPONGE

*A fatless sponge, flavoured with ginger and cocoa,
sandwiched with cream and crystallised ginger.*

2 oz. cornflour
2 level tablespoons flour
2 level teaspoons ground ginger
2 level teaspoons ground cinnamon
2 level teaspoons cocoa powder
1 level teaspoon bicarbonate of soda

2 level teaspoons cream of tartar
1 dessertspoon warmed golden syrup
4 eggs, separated
4 oz. sugar
Whipped cream
Crystallised ginger

Set oven to 350°F or Mark 4. Grease and flour two deep 7 inch sandwich tins. Sift the flours and spices, cocoa, bicarbonate of soda and cream of tartar together four times to mix them thoroughly. In a bowl, whisk the egg whites until stiff then gradually add the sugar, whisking well after each addition. Add the egg yolks all at once. Sift the flour mixture on to eggs and sugar mixture and fold in gently. Pour in the warmed syrup and mix in. Pour into the tins and bake for 15-20 minutes until firm. Turn out on to a wire rack. When cool, sandwich together with whipped cream and chopped crystallised ginger. Eat the same day.

— TERRY WHITWORTH —

HONEY GINGERBREAD

A traditional, dark gingerbread, with the addition of honey and cinnamon.

4 oz. butter	½ teaspoon salt
4 oz. sugar	1 teaspoon cinnamon
1 egg, beaten	1 teaspoon ground ginger
10 oz. flour	6 tablespoons black treacle
1 teaspoon bicarbonate of soda	6 tablespoons clear honey
	6 fl.oz. hot water

Set oven to 350°F or Mark 4. Grease and line a shallow 9 inch x 9 inch baking tin. Melt the butter in a pan and allow to cool. Beat together the sugar and egg and add to the butter. Combine together the flour, bicarbonate of soda, salt and spices. In a separate bowl mix together the treacle, honey and water. Add the dry and the liquid ingredients alternately to the butter mixture, blending well after each addition. Put into the tin and bake for one hour. Leave to cool for 10 minutes then turn out on to a wire rack.

NUT AND APPLE CAKE

This coffee and nut sponge cake has an apple and apricot jam filling.

4 oz. butter	4 oz. self-raising flour
4 oz. caster sugar	Pinch of salt
2 eggs, separated	1 teaspoon instant coffee
1½ oz. roasted ground hazelnuts	1 tablespoon warm milk

Filling:

1 lb. Cox's Orange Pippin apples	Rind and juice of ½ lemon
2 tablespoons apricot jam	2 oz. melted plain chocolate or sifted icing sugar for topping

Set oven to 375°F or Mark 5. Grease and line an 8 inch round cake tin. Soften the butter in a bowl, add the sugar and beat until fluffy. Add the egg yolks, nuts, sifted flour and salt. Dissolve the coffee in the milk and add to the mixture; fold in the stiffly beaten egg whites. Turn into the prepared tin and bake for about 25 minutes until firm to the touch. Turn on to a wire rack and leave to cool. Meanwhile peel, core and slice the apples and place in a pan with the jam and the rind and juice of ½ lemon. Cover and cook gently until soft. Cool. Split the cake in half and fill with the apple mixture. For the top of the cake, either spread with 2 oz of melted plain chocolate or sprinkle with sifted icing sugar.

ORANGE AND WALNUT CAKE

A plain cake flavoured with orange juice and marmalade.

6 oz. butter, softened   Grated rind of an orange
5 tablespoons water and orange juice, mixed   6 oz. caster sugar
Water icing:
2 eggs, separated   10 oz. flour   1 teaspoon baking powder
2 oz. orange marmalade   3 oz. chopped walnuts
Made with sifted icing sugar and sufficient water and strained orange juice
to give a light coating consistency
Walnut halves to decorate

Set oven to 350°F or Mark 4. Grease and flour a round 7 inch cake tin and line the base. Cream together in a bowl the butter, orange rind and sugar until light and fluffy, then beat in the egg yolks. Sift the flour and baking powder together and fold in. Add the marmalade, chopped walnuts and the water/orange juice mixture and combine lightly. Whisk the egg whites until they stand in soft peaks and fold into the mixture. Turn into the tin and smooth over lightly. Bake for 1 to 1¼ hours, or until a skewer inserted into the cake comes out clean, covering with foil if it appears to be browning too quickly. Allow to stand in the tin for 5 to 10 minutes, then turn out and cool on a wire rack. When completely cold, lightly brush off the top of the cake and drizzle over it the water icing; decorate with walnut halves.

RICH PLUM CAKE

A celebration cake full of dried fruit and flavoured with rum or brandy.

½ lb. butter	½ lb. raisins
½ lb. caster sugar	½ lb. sultanas
6 medium eggs, lightly beaten	½ lb. candied peel
½ lb. flour	½ lb. almonds, blanched and chopped
½ lb. currants	2 tablespoons rum or brandy
¼ lb. glacé cherries	1 tablespoon black coffee

Set oven to 325°F or Mark 3. Grease an 8 inch cake tin. Cream together the butter and sugar in a bowl. Add the lightly beaten eggs, one at a time, with a teaspoon of flour after the third egg. Beat thoroughly. Mix all the fruit together with half the flour. Stir the rest of the flour, with the peel and almonds, into the egg and butter mixture. Then add the floured fruit, the rum or brandy and the coffee and mix well. Place in the tin and bake for 2½ hours or longer until a skewer pushed into the cake comes out clean. To prevent the sides from browning, tie a band of brown paper round the outside of the tin. Leave to cool for about 10 minutes and turn out on to a wire rack.

-TERRY WHITWORTH-

BUTTERMILK SCONES

*Scones made with buttermilk are much lighter
and tastier than those made with fresh milk.*

8 oz. flour

1 teaspoon bicarbonate of soda

1 teaspoon cream of tartar

Pinch of salt

1 oz. butter

7 fl.oz. buttermilk
   (or a little more or less)

Milk to glaze

Set oven to 425°F or Mark 7. Lightly grease and flour a baking sheet. Sieve the dry ingredients into a mixing bowl. Rub in the butter until the mixture resembles fine breadcrumbs. Make a well in the centre and pour in almost all the buttermilk. Using a broad bladed knife, quickly stir the buttermilk into the flour to form a soft dough, adding more buttermilk if needed. Turn out on to a lightly floured surface and roll or pat out to ¾ inch thickness. Cut into rounds using a 2½ inch cutter and place on the baking sheet. Brush the tops with milk to glaze. Bake for 15 to 20 minutes until well risen and light golden brown. Serve with butter and jam. Best eaten the same day.

APPLE CAKE

A simple, plain cake which is kept moist by the apple pieces.

8 oz. self-raising flour	**4 oz. caster sugar**
4 oz. butter	**Grated rind of 1 lemon**
½ lb cooking apples,	**1 medium egg, beaten**
peeled, cored and diced	**2 oz. sultanas (optional)**

Set oven to 375°F or Mark 5. Grease and line an 8 inch round cake tin. Put the flour into a mixing bowl and rub in the butter until the mixture resembles fine breadcrumbs. Stir in the apples, sugar, lemon rind and egg and mix well. Add the sultanas, if desired. Put the mixture into the cake tin and bake for 30 to 40 minutes until golden in colour and a skewer inserted comes out clean. Serve warm as a pudding with custard or cold, spread with butter.

- TERRY WHITWORTH -

NUT CAKE

A rich cake that is chock full of nuts and flavour.

6 oz. butter	½ teaspoon ground cinnamon
4 oz. soft brown sugar	2 eggs, beaten
4 oz. self-raising wholemeal flour	8 oz. chopped hazelnuts or walnuts, or mixed

Set oven to 350°F or Mark 4. Grease and line a 7 inch square cake tin. Melt the butter in a pan over a low heat, stir in the sugar until it dissolves then remove from the heat and cool slightly. Sieve the flour and cinnamon into a mixing bowl, make a well in the centre and pour in the butter/sugar mixture. Add the beaten eggs, stir in the nuts and mix well. Put into the cake tin and bake for 30 to 45 minutes until golden brown. Test that a skewer inserted comes out clean. Cover with greaseproof paper if the top appears to be browning too quickly. Cool in the tin.

SALLY LUNNS TEACAKES

There are lots of versions of this famous teacake; many include butter in the dough. This recipe uses cream instead, which gives a smoother, lighter result, close to the original recipe.

**½ oz. fresh yeast   4 tablespoons lukewarm milk   1 lb. strong white flour
2 teaspoons salt   1 teaspoon ground mixed spice
8-10 fl.oz. thick double (or clotted) cream, at room temperature
4 eggs, beaten   2 tablespoons sugar dissolved in 2 tablespoons milk to glaze**

Crumble the yeast into the milk in a cup and leave for a few minutes until frothy. Meanwhile mix the flour, salt and spice in a large mixing bowl. Add the yeast mixture, cream and eggs and mix until thick - just stiff enough to form into shape. Halve the dough and form each half into a ball. Place each ball of dough into a buttered, floured 6 inch round, deep cake tin and sprinkle each lightly with flour. Cover with a clean tea towel and leave in a warm place until the dough has risen to the tops of the tins; about 1½ to 2 hours. Meanwhile, set oven to 400°F or Mark 6. When risen, immediately place the cake tins in the pre-heated oven and bake for 15 minutes until golden. Heat the milk and sugar for the glaze in a small pan until boiling. Brush the top of each cake with this mixture while still in the tin. Cool in the tin for a few minutes then turn out and split the cakes in half. Spread with clotted cream or butter, replace the tops and eat while warm. Alternatively leave plain and eat with ice cream or a fruit dessert.

CHESTNUT SHORTBREAD

These soft, shortbread biscuits are golden brown with a spicy, nutty flavour.

6 oz. chestnuts	**4 oz. butter, softened**
¼ pt milk	**2 oz. honey**
2 inch piece cinnamon stick	**1 teaspoon ground cinnamon**
6 oz. wholemeal flour	

Set oven to 350°F or Mark 4. Skin the chestnuts by making a small slit in the skin, cover with boiling water and leave for 5 minutes. Peel off the outer and inner skins while still warm. Put the peeled nuts into a pan with the milk and cinnamon stick. Bring slowly to the boil and simmer, covered, for about 20 minutes until the milk is absorbed. Put the chestnuts into a mixing bowl and mash to a pulp. Beat the chopped butter with the chestnuts then mix in the honey and ground cinnamon. Fold in the flour and work, with the fingers, to make a soft dough. Turn out on to a floured surface and roll out to ¼ inch thickness. Cut out 2½ inch rounds with a cutter and lay on a floured baking sheet. Bake for 15 minutes until golden brown but still soft. Transfer very carefully on to a wire rack to cool.

CUMBERLAND BUTTERMILK CAKE

An old farmhouse recipe originally made using surplus buttermilk.

1 lb. flour	8 oz. candied peel, chopped
6 oz. butter	4 oz. sultanas
4 oz. caster sugar	1 teaspoon bicarbonate of soda
2 generous tablespoons orange marmalade	5 fl.oz. buttermilk, heated to lukewarm

Set oven to 325°F or Mark 3. Grease and line an 8 inch round cake tin. Sift the flour into a mixing bowl and rub in the butter until the mixture resembles breadcrumbs. Stir in the sugar, marmalade, peel and sultanas. Stir the bicarbonate of soda into the lukewarm buttermilk and add to the cake mixture. Mix to a soft dough (it may be necessary to add a little more buttermilk) and put into the cake tin. Bake for 1 hour, then reduce the temperature to 300°F or Mark 2 and bake for another 45 minutes or until a skewer inserted comes out clean. Cool in the tin for 10 minutes then turn out on to a wire rack to finish cooling.

The Langdale Pikes, Lake District, Cumbria

-TERRY WHITWORTH-

CHERRY TART

Really ripe cherries, harvested in July, make this delicious, open tart. For convenience, tinned cherries may be used but they will slightly lack the full, cherry flavour of freshly picked fruit.

Pastry:
8 oz. flour   Pinch of salt   1 oz. cornflour
2 level teaspoons icing sugar   4 oz. lard and margarine mixed
1 egg yolk   2 tablespoons cold water
Filling:
1 lb. black cherries, stoned (if using canned cherries, drain well)
4 oz. icing sugar   3 oz. ground almonds
2 eggs   Almond essence

Set oven to 400°F or Mark 6. Sift the flour, salt, cornflour and icing sugar into a mixing bowl. Rub in the mixed fat and bind to a dough with the egg yolk and water. Knead the pastry lightly and roll out on a floured surface. Line a 9 inch fluted flan ring on a greased baking sheet with the pastry. Bake blind for 15 minutes. Reduce the oven temperature to 325°F or Mark 3. Arrange the cherries in the pastry case. Mix the icing sugar, eggs and almonds together with a little almond essence and pour the mixture over the cherries. Bake for 50 to 60 minutes until firm and golden. Serve hot or cold with cream.

Eighteen

LEEK AND MUSHROOM TART

Leeks are an excellent source of vitamin C, iron and fibre. Choose small or medium size leeks, less than an inch diameter, with fresh green leaf tops.

8 inch, baked shortcrust pastry flan case   2 medium leeks
1 oz. butter   4 oz. sliced mushrooms   Salt and pepper
2 eggs   5 fl.oz. milk   6 oz. Edam cheese, grated

Set oven to 350°F or Mark 4. Trim leeks and slice into ½ inch rings, washing well. Heat the butter in a pan, add the leeks, cover and cook for 10 minutes. Add the mushrooms and seasoning and cook for 5 minutes. Use a slotted spoon to remove the vegetables and place them in the flan case. Beat the eggs and milk in a bowl and season well. Add the cheese and sprinkle over the vegetables. Bake for 30 minutes until set and golden brown. Serves 4.

— TERRY WHITWORTH

STILTON TART

This distinctive English cheese with its creamy texture and tangy flavour combines well with the peppery flavour of the watercress.

1 lb. shortcrust pastry   1 oz. unsalted butter
A bunch of spring onions, trimmed and chopped into 2 inch lengths
4 oz. frozen peas   5 fl.oz. single cream   4 medium eggs, beaten
A bunch of watercress, trimmed and roughly chopped
5 oz. Stilton, cut into ¼ inch cubes   Salt and pepper
12 cherry tomatoes, halved

Set oven to 400°F or Mark 6. Line a 10 inch greased flan tin with the pastry. Prick the base with a fork, cover with greaseproof paper and baking beans and bake blind for 10 minutes. Remove paper and beans and return pastry case to oven for 5-10 minutes until cooked and crisp. Remove from oven and allow to cool slightly. Lower oven temperature to 350°F or Mark 4. Melt butter in a pan, add onions and peas, stirring over low heat for 30 seconds. Cover and cook for 3-4 minutes until softened. Remove from heat and set aside to cool. Meanwhile, in a bowl, combine the cream, eggs, half of the watercress and half of the Stilton. Season, add onions and peas, stirring well. Spoon into pastry case and distribute tomato halves evenly across the top. Sprinkle rest of Stilton over the top and cook for 30-35 minutes until set and browned. Serve warm or cold garnished with remaining watercress. Serves 4.

The Square, Hope Cove, South Devon

CHEESE, TOMATO AND BACON TART

Cheese tarts in various forms make versatile and satisfying dishes which taste good eaten cold or hot. Smoked bacon would add to the flavour, if preferred.

8 oz. shortcrust pastry	2 eggs, beaten
Cooking oil	¼ pint milk
6 oz. streaky bacon, cut into pieces	Freshly ground black pepper
1 large onion, roughly chopped	2 oz. Cheddar cheese, grated
1 clove garlic, crushed	2 tomatoes, sliced into wheels

A sprinkling of oregano or basil

Set oven to 375°F or Mark 5. Butter a 9 inch flan dish. Roll out the pastry on a floured surface and line the dish. Trim the edge. Prick the pastry all over with a fork and bake blind for about 10 minutes. Meanwhile, heat a little oil in a frying pan and fry the bacon and onion together with the garlic until the bacon is cooked and the onion is soft but not brown. Arrange the bacon, onion and garlic over the pastry base. In a jug, mix the beaten eggs with the milk and some twists of pepper and stir in half of the grated cheese. Pour the mixture over the bacon and onion. Arrange the tomato wheels over the top and sprinkle over the remaining grated cheese with a little oregano or basil. Bake for about 25 minutes until the topping is set. Serves 4 to 6.

SAVOURY CHICKEN TART

A useful picnic recipe or standby meal when pressed for time.
Cooked chicken left-overs may be added.

8 oz. shortcrust pastry
1 large tomato, sliced
1 can condensed cream of chicken soup
2 eggs, beaten   Milk or water
Salt and pepper

Set oven to 425°F or Mark 7. Roll out pastry and use to line a 7 inch flan dish. Cover the bottom of the flan with slices of tomato. Tip can of condensed soup into a measuring jug, add eggs and top up to ¾ pint with the milk or water. Season to taste with salt and freshly ground black pepper and pour carefully into pastry case. Bake for 15 minutes then reduce heat to 375°F or Mark 5 and bake until the filling is set and the pastry is crispy. Serve with sliced tomato and a green salad. Serves 6.

EGG CUSTARD FLAN

One of the earliest flan recipes and one which is still popular today.

6 oz. shortcrust pastry   **1-2 oz golden caster sugar**
2 large eggs   **10 fl.oz. milk**
Grated nutmeg (optional)

Set oven to 425°F or Mark 7. Roll out the pastry on a floured surface and line a 7 inch round flan tin about 1 inch deep. Whisk the eggs lightly with the sugar. Heat the milk in a pan until warm and pour on to the eggs, whisking lightly. Strain into the flan case and sprinkle with nutmeg if using. Bake in the centre of the oven for 10 minutes, then reduce the temperature to 350°F or Mark 4 and bake for another 20 to 25 minutes until the custard is set. Serves 4.

- TERRY WHITWORTH -

TOMATO AND BASIL QUICHE

A favourite traditional brunch, quiche is usually served at room temperature or chilled.

6 oz. shortcrust pastry   1 oz. butter   1 onion, sliced thinly
5 large tomatoes, skinned and sliced thinly   ¼ pint single cream
3 eggs   2 oz. grated Cheddar cheese
2 tablespoons chopped fresh basil   Salt and pepper

Set oven to 400°F or Mark 6. Roll out pastry and use to line a 9 inch flan case. Melt the butter in a frying pan, add the onion and fry for 5 minutes. Remove from pan and spread over bottom of flan case. Arrange the tomatoes over the onions. Combine the cream, eggs and cheese, stir in the basil, and season to taste. Pour mixture over the tomatoes, place dish on a baking sheet and bake for 40 minutes until the filling is firm and golden brown. Serves 4-6.

OLD ENGLISH CHEESECAKE

This is adapted from an early medieval recipe. It is best eaten the day it is made.

8 oz. shortcrust pastry	4 egg yolks
Pinch of saffron strands	2 oz. caster sugar
1 tablespoon very hot water	Pinch ground ginger
12 oz. full fat soft cheese	Freshly grated nutmeg
(e.g. Brie or similar)	Pinch of salt

Set oven to 375°F or Mark 5. Line an 8 inch flan tin or dish with the pastry. Soak the saffron strands in the hot water until the liquid is deep gold in colour. Meanwhile, beat the cheese in a bowl until smooth and creamy. In another bowl whisk the egg yolks with the sugar until thick and pale and then gradually beat in the cheese. Stir in the spices, salt and saffron liquid. Turn into the pastry case and bake for 20 to 25 minutes until just set in the middle. Serve warm or cold. Serves 4.

- TERRY WHITWORTH -

CHEESE AND POTATO BAKE

A dish comprised of layered cheese and potatoes; a useful supper dish.

2-4 oz. butter
6 medium potatoes, peeled and cut into thin slices
2 medium onions, peeled and thinly sliced

Salt and black pepper
2 cloves garlic, peeled and crushed
4 oz. Cheddar cheese, grated
1 pint full cream milk

Set oven to 325°F or Mark 3. Butter a large, shallow ovenproof dish, arrange a layer of sliced potatoes over the base and spread over a layer of sliced onion. Dot with butter, sprinkle with salt and black pepper, add a little crushed garlic and sprinkle over about one quarter of the cheese. Continue making layers like this, finishing with a layer of potatoes topped with cheese. Pour on the milk and cover the dish with kitchen foil. Cook for 1¼ hours, remove the foil and continue cooking for a further 30 minutes until the potatoes are tender. This is an excellent accompaniment to many meat dishes, but also makes a light supper dish served on its own.

CHEESE PUDDING

A light, baked pudding of breadcrumbs, eggs and grated cheese.

1 oz. butter	¾ pint milk
1 cup of fresh breadcrumbs, brown or white	2 eggs, beaten
	Dash of Worcestershire sauce
1 small onion, finely chopped	1 teaspoon made mustard
	3 tomatoes, sliced
Salt and black pepper	Chopped chives or parsley
6 oz. strong grated cheese	for decoration

Set oven to 350°F or Mark 4. Grease a casserole dish with butter. Mix the bread-crumbs, onions, salt, pepper and 4 oz of the cheese in the casserole. Pour the milk on to the beaten eggs, add the Worcestershire sauce and mustard and mix together. Pour over the breadcrumb mixture. Sprinkle the rest of the cheese on top. Cover with the sliced tomatoes. Sprinkle with black pepper and dot with butter. Bake for about one hour until firm and golden. Decorate with chopped chives or parsley. Serve with watercress or endive and crusty wholemeal rolls. Serves 4.

EGG AND CHEESE PIE

A shortcrust pastry flan case filled with grated cheese and whole eggs,
with a crispy breadcrumb topping.

4 oz. shortcrust pastry	Salt and pepper
8 oz. Cheddar cheese, grated	1 oz. fresh brown breadcrumbs
4 eggs	Butter for dotting
2 tablespoons milk	

Set oven to 400°F or Mark 6. Grease a 7 inch flan dish. Roll out the pastry on a floured surface, line the dish and trim the edge. Prick the bottom with a fork, line with a circle of greaseproof paper, fill with baking beans and bake blind for about 10 to 12 minutes. Remove the beans and paper, return to the oven and cook for about a further 6 to 8 minutes until baked through. Allow to cool. Reduce oven to 350°F or Mark 4. Spread half the cheese over the base of the flan case and in it make 4 hollows. Carefully break an egg into each hollow and season. Cover with the remaining cheese and then with the breadcrumbs. Dot with butter and sprinkle all over with the milk to moisten. Bake for about 30 to 45 minutes until set and browned on top. Serve with sliced tomatoes. Serves 4.

BLACKBERRY PIE

There is nothing more redolent of autumn than blackberries picked from the hedgerow and made into this succulent pie.

10 oz. shortcrust pastry
1 lb. blackberries, rinsed and drained very well and any stalks removed
4 oz. soft brown sugar   ½ level teaspoon ground cinnamon or nutmeg
A walnut of butter   1 tablespoon sherry
Milk or beaten egg to glaze

Set oven to 400°F or Mark 6. Lightly butter a 10 inch pie plate. Roll out the pastry on a lightly floured surface and use half to line the pie plate. Layer the blackberries and the sugar blended with the spice, over the pastry base. Dot with the walnut of butter and then sprinkle over the sherry. Cover with the remaining pastry, trimming the edges and sealing well. Decorate with the pastry trimmings and make a small steam hole in the centre. Brush with a little milk or beaten egg to glaze and cook for about 30 to 35 minutes or until the pastry is golden. Serve hot with cream. Serves 4-6.

Exmoor cottage at Selworthy, Somerset

PUMPKIN PIE

Many people assume this recipe to be American, but in fact it is English and dates from Tudor times. The early colonists introduced pumpkin to America where it quickly became a national dish, while here in England pumpkin fell from favour in the eighteenth century.

1 can pumpkin purée (450g approximately)
Pinch of salt
4 oz. soft brown sugar
1 teaspoon ground cinnamon
½ teaspoon ground ginger
¼ teaspoon grated nutmeg
2 eggs beaten
5 fl.oz. single cream
8 oz. shortcrust pastry

Set oven to 375°F or Mark 5. Grease an 8 inch pie dish or flan tin. Put the pumpkin purée with the salt, sugar and spices into a mixing bowl and combine together. Add the eggs and cream and stir well to mix. Roll out the pastry on a floured surface and use to line the pie dish or flan tin. Pour in the filling, spread out evenly and bake for 45 to 55 minutes until a knife inserted in the filling comes out clean. Allow to cool. Serve warm or cold with cream.

DAMSON PIE

Damsons harvested from the hedgerows, together with orange and mace, give this pie a rich, traditional flavour.

Pastry:
8 oz. wholemeal flour   2 oz. lard   3 oz. butter
1 teaspoon baking powder   Pinch of salt
4 tablespoons cold water   Beaten egg to glaze

Filling:
1 lb. damsons   Pinch ground mace
Grated rind and juice large orange   4 tablespoons honey
2 tablespoons tapioca or sago

First make the pastry and set aside in a cool place. Stone the damsons and put into a pan with the orange rind and juice, mace and honey. Set over a low heat, cover and cook gently for 15 minutes to become very juicy. Remove from the heat and mix in the tapioca or sago. Set aside and leave to cool. Set oven to 400°F or Mark 6. Roll out the pastry on a floured surface and use two thirds to line a deep 7 inch flan dish. Put in the damson mixture, cover with a pastry lid, seal the edges, brush with beaten egg and make a small steam hole. Bake for 30 minutes until golden brown. Serve hot or cold with whipped or clotted cream.

- TERRY WHITWORTH -

COUNTRY PORK PIE

Ideal for a buffet or summer picnic. Serve with English mustard and a mixed salad.

18 oz. shortcrust pastry
6 oz. bacon, rinds removed, minced
1½ lb. lean minced pork
1 onion, peeled and chopped
12 oz. pork sausagemeat

2 tbsp. Worcestershire sauce
1 teaspoon dried sage
Salt & freshly ground black pepper
4 hard-boiled eggs
Beaten egg for glazing

Set oven to 400°F or Mark 6. Roll out two thirds of the pastry and use to line a greased 8 inch circular loose-bottomed cake tin. Mix together remaining ingredients except for the eggs. Place half of this mixture in the lined tin, place the eggs on top and cover with the rest of the pork mixture. Roll out the rest of the pastry to make a lid. Moisten the edges of the pastry, cover with the lid and seal the edges well. Trim off any excess pastry and make a slit in the centre. Decorate the top with any remaining pastry. Glaze with the beaten egg. Bake in the oven for 1½ hours, covering the top with foil after half an hour to avoid excess browning. Allow to cool in the tin before removing. Serves 8-10.

SMOKED HADDOCK AND CHEESE FLAN

A tasty creamy flan which can also be made with milk instead of cream, herrings or kippers and or dry grated cheese instead of the cottage cheese for a more thrifty version.

8 oz. smoked haddock	8 inch baked pastry flan case
5 fl.oz. water	2 eggs, beaten
Juice of ½ lemon	6 tablespoons single cream
1 oz. butter	4 oz. cottage cheese
1 onion, chopped finely	1 tablespoon chopped fresh parsley
2 oz. button mushrooms, chopped	Salt and pepper

Set oven to 375°F or Mark 5. Place haddock, water and half the lemon juice in a pan and poach fish. Drain, remove skin and bones and flake the flesh. Melt the butter in a pan, add onion and cook for 2 minutes then add chopped mushrooms and cook for a further 4 minutes. Combine the fish and vegetables and spoon over base of pastry case. Add the cream, cheese lemon juice and parsley to the beaten eggs. Season to taste. Pour into pastry case and bake in the preheated oven for 30-35 minutes until set and browned. Serves 4-6.

STEAK AND KIDNEY PIE

A distinctive British dish, often made as a one-crust pie, where the filling is covered but not completely enclosed by the pastry.

1 oz. flour   Salt and pepper   1½ lb. stewing steak cubed
6 oz. ox kidney, cores removed and cubed   1 oz. butter
1 large onion peeled and chopped   1 bayleaf   1 tablespoon Worcestershire sauce
1 tablespoon tomato purée   ¼ pint beef stock
¼ pint brown ale   9 oz. shortcrust pastry   Beaten egg for glazing

Season flour with salt and pepper. Roll meat in flour and shake well. Reserve remaining flour. Melt butter in a large pan, add chopped onion and cook for 3 minutes stirring occasionally. Increase heat add meat and seal. Add remaining flour and cook for 2-3 minutes, stirring frequently. Add bayleaf, Worcestershire sauce, tomato purée, then slowly pour in stock and ale, bring to the boil stirring constantly. Cover, reduce heat to a bare simmer and cook for 1½-2 hours. Set oven to 400°F or Mark 6. Transfer cooked meat to a 3 pint pie dish. Roll out pastry so that it is 2 inches larger than the dish and cut off a ½ inch strip from around the outside. Dampen the edge of the pie dish and place strip around the lip. Moisten pastry strip and cover the pie with remaining pastry lid. Ensuring edges are sealed, knock back and trim off excess. Shape trimmings and use to decorate top of pie. Brush with beaten egg to glaze and cook for 35-40 minutes in oven. Serves 4.

CHICKEN PICNIC PIE

*Marinated chicken strips are layered with sausagemeat
and topped with a pastry lid.*

**8 oz. shortcrust pastry chilled
1½ lbs. boneless chicken cut into ½ strips
1 teaspoon mace   Salt and ground black pepper
Juice and rind of a lemon   1 lb. pork sausagemeat
6 spring onions, chopped   1 teaspoon fresh thyme
1 tablespoon fresh sage   2 tablespoons double cream
Beaten egg for glazing**

Set oven to 400°F or Mark 6. Use half the pastry to line a greased round 8 inch diameter sloping sided pie dish. Marinate the chicken strips with the mace, seasoning and a little lemon juice. Mix the sausagemeat, spring onions, herbs, lemon rind and 2 tablespoon lemon juice together. Pour in the cream, mixing well. Put one third of this mixture in the pastry base, spread flat and cover with half the chicken. Add a second layer of sausagemeat, followed by the remaining chicken and finally the third layer of sausagemeat. Roll out the remaining pastry and cover the pie. Moisten and seal the edges well. Glaze with the beaten egg and bake for 30 minutes. Reduce the heat to 350°F or Mark 4 and cook for another 1¼ hours. Serves 6-8.

Gold Hill, Shaftesbury, Dorset

-TERRY WHITWORTH-

CHEESE CRUST VEGETABLE PIE

Tasty garden vegetables wrapped in a savoury cheese pastry.

Cheese Pastry: 6 oz. flour   ½ teaspoon salt   ½ teaspoon dried mustard powder
4 oz. butter   3 oz. Cheddar cheese, finely grated   Water
Vegetable filling: 3 medium carrots, peeled and diced   6 oz. corn kernels
2 medium onions, finely diced   1 clove garlic, crushed
½ medium swede, peeled and diced   2 oz. fresh peas
Sauce: 1½ oz. margarine   1½ oz. flour   ¾ pint of milk
Dried mixed herbs to taste   Salt and pepper

Prepare the pastry by the traditional rubbing-in method or in a food processor. Place in the refrigerator to rest. Set oven to 375°F or Mark 5. Place all the vegetables, except the peas, in a large saucepan with 2–3 tablespoons of water, cover and cook gently until tender. Stir in the peas. Make the sauce by melting the margarine, adding the flour and cooking for 2–3 minutes. Remove from the heat and gradually add the milk, beating well between each addition. Return to the heat and, stirring continuously, bring to the boil. Add the vegetables to the sauce with the mixed herbs and season well. Put into a pie dish and immediately cover with the cheese pastry. Bake until the pastry is golden in colour; 35 minutes approximately. The vegetables in this pie can be varied according to what is in season.

RAISED VEAL AND HAM PIE

The pastry is mixed with boiling water, making a pliable dough which can be moulded into a raised pie that holds its shape.

Pastry: 1 lb. plain flour   2 teaspoons salt   4 oz. lard   9 fl. oz. water
Filling: ¾ lb. diced pie veal   4 oz. chopped ham   1 tablespoon chopped parsley
Grated rind and juice of a lemon   Salt and pepper   A little water   1 hard boiled egg
Beaten egg to glaze   Jelly stock (2 tablespoons gelatine dissolved in ½ pint chicken stock)

Set oven to 425°F or Mark 7. Mix flour and salt and make a well in the centre. Melt lard in water, boil and pour into well. Beat quickly with a wooden spoon to a soft dough. Knead until smooth. Cover with a damp teatowel and leave to rest for 30 minutes. Roll out ⅔ of pastry into an 11x10 inch oval. Grease a round cake tin, drape pastry over rolling pin and unroll over tin. (Keep remaining pastry covered with a damp cloth.) Press into tin and raise to ¼ inch above the rim. Mix veal, ham, parsley, lemon rind and juice, season to taste and add a little water to moisten. Half fill pastry case with meat mixture, place egg in the centre, add remaining meat and cover with rest of pastry rolled to fit the top. Pinch edges together and flute. Glaze with beaten egg combined with a little water. Make a small hole in centre with a sharp knife. Tie a band of greaseproof paper around pie. Cook for 15-20 minutes then reduce heat to 350°F or Mark 4 and cook for a further 1½ hours until meat is tender. When cold, fill pie with jelly stock. Leave to set.

- TERRY WHITWORTH -

LAMB AND APPLE PIE

A tasty meal served with creamed potatoes and carrots,
this dish is called Squab Pie in the Cotswolds.

8 oz. shortcrust pastry
12 small best-end-of-neck lamb cutlets
1 large cooking apple, peeled, cored and sliced
2 onions, peeled and sliced   Salt and black pepper
½ teaspoon ground nutmeg   ¼ pint lamb stock
Milk or beaten egg to glaze

Set oven to 400°F or Mark 6. Place half the lamb in a 1½ to 2 pint pie dish and layer half the apple and onion slices on top. Sprinkle with seasoning and nutmeg, then place the remainder of the lamb and the apple and onion slices on top. Pour on the stock. Roll out the pastry on a lightly floured surface and cover the pie, trimming the edges neatly and sealing well. Use trimmings for decoration and make a small 'steam hole' in the centre of the lid. Brush with milk or beaten egg to glaze. Bake for 20 minutes, then lower the oven temperature to 350°F or Mark 4 and cook for a further 1 to 1¼ hours. Serves 4.

Cotswold cottages at Broadway, Worcestershire

PORK AND CHESTNUT PIE

Light and tasty, this pie combines the traditional flavours of Christmas.

Pastry:
12 oz. flour   4 oz. butter   2 oz. lard   ½ teaspoon salt   3 fl.oz. water
Filling:
1 tablespoon cooking oil   1 small onion, finely chopped
12 oz. pork fillet, chopped roughly
12 oz. tinned whole chestnuts, chopped roughly
1 teaspoon chopped thyme   1 teaspoon chopped sage
Salt and pepper   3 eggs, beaten   12 oz. cranberries

In a bowl, rub the fats into the flour and stir in the salt. Mix to a dough with the cold water, wrap in cling film and chill for 1 hour. Set oven to 400°F or Mark 6. Heat the oil in a pan and cook the onions until soft but not browned. Place the pork and chestnuts in a large bowl and add the onion. Stir in the herbs and seasoning to taste and mix well. Beat 2 eggs and add to the bowl with the cranberries, stirring thoroughly to combine. Roll out two thirds of the pastry on a floured surface and line a loose based 9½ inch flan tin. Fill with the pork mixture, smoothing it out evenly. Roll out the rest of the pastry to make a lid, cover and seal the edges with water. Beat the remaining egg and brush over the pie to glaze. Bake for 40-50 minutes. Serve hot or cold.

GARDENER'S PIE

Courgettes are the basis of this vegetable crumble,
which has cheese and mixed nuts in the topping.

3 tablespoons walnut oil   2 onions, peeled and sliced
3 cloves of garlic, peeled and crushed
2 lb. courgettes, washed, trimmed and cut into ½ inch slices
1 lb. tomatoes, skinned and chopped   2 tablespoons tomato purée
3 or 4 basil leaves, chopped   Salt and pepper
Topping:
3 oz. fresh brown breadcrumbs
2 oz. Cheddar cheese, grated
2 oz. chopped mixed nuts

Set oven to 350°F or Mark 4. Heat the oil in a large saucepan, add the onions
and garlic and cook gently for 5 minutes. Add all the remaining ingredients,
season and cook for a further 5 minutes. Turn into a 3 pint ovenproof dish.
Topping: mix together the topping ingredients and sprinkle evenly over the
vegetables. Cook in the oven for about 30 minutes. Serve hot with crusty
bread. Serves 4.

METRIC CONVERSIONS

The weights, measures and oven temperatures used in the preceding recipes can be easily converted to their metric equivalents. The conversions listed below are only approximate, having been rounded up or down as may be appropriate.

Weights

Avoirdupois	Metric
1 oz.	just under 30 grams
4 oz. (¼ lb.)	app. 115 grams
8 oz. (½ lb.)	app. 230 grams
1 lb.	454 grams

Liquid Measures

Imperial	Metric
1 tablespoon (liquid only)	20 millilitres
1 fl. oz.	app. 30 millilitres
1 gill (¼ pt.)	app. 145 millilitres
½ pt.	app. 285 millilitres
1 pt.	app. 570 millilitres
1 qt.	app. 1.140 litres

Oven Temperatures

	°Fahrenheit	Gas Mark	°Celsius
Slow	300	2	150
	325	3	170
Moderate	350	4	180
	375	5	190
	400	6	200
Hot	425	7	220
	450	8	230
	475	9	240

Flour as specified in these recipes refers to plain flour unless otherwise described.